MARNI PENNING

The Penning Method for the Panicked Actor

*The Anxious Actor's Guide
to Easily Creating Memorable, Confident,
and Specific Performances
in Last-Minute Auditions*

To Jesse
Pencils have erasers for a reason —
You can always change your mind.

"Mark but the Penning of it."

— WILLIAM SHAKESPEARE

WELCOME TO

THE PENNING METHOD
for the Panicked Actor

This simple, infinitely repeatable and adaptable technique is named after me—Marni Penning, award-winning actress and audiobook narrator—and if you've picked up this tiny book, chances are that I've been where you are now.

Let me tell you a little story...

Once upon a time, as a young actor in New York, I walked into an audition and was handed a monologue that I had never seen before. The director said, "Look that over, and we'll see you in about five minutes."

The piece was thick with wild imagery and non-sequiturs, and repetition at the beginning of almost every sentence. I looked at it and thought, "FIVE MINUTES?!?!?"

But I pulled out my pencil and got to work. And five minutes later, I was able to wow the director with a unique, memorable, confident performance... and I got the job.

And now I'll teach you the techniques I used, so you can do it, too!

(BECAUSE IT SURE HAS BEEN ME!)

- Do you <u>freeze</u> with overwhelm?
- Do you *panic* when someone hands you material you feel you don't have time to prepare thoroughly?
- Do you question your choices?
- Whenever you audition, do you always think you could have done it better?
- Can you get mired in self-doubt, sometimes having a hard time letting go of a "bad" audition?

Me too! I freeze up when I rely on my memory and don't commit my choices to the script.

But as soon as I began using this method to quickly notate my choices, I was able to perform freely, without self-doubt, knowing I made the best, most unique choices I could in the time I was allotted.

And then I go out and get myself a cup of tea to celebrate and move on to the next thing. You can, too! Let the marks guide you so you can just PLAY!

So... Why THE "PENNING" METHOD?

I always tell people my last name is, "Penning... like writing things down."

How fitting, then, that this method would be all about "Penning" your unique marks to shape your script so you'll never lose your place, you'll always know exactly what you mean, and you'll wow them with your confidence!

All from a little "Penning."

I started performing onstage when I was 8 years old. (My family will tell you I was performing *long* before that.)

I had a wonderful fourth grade teacher who introduced me to Shakespeare and changed my life. So since that time, I've always used Shakespearean notation to mark my scripts for clarity and stresses.

It dawned on me that this kind of notation, with a little tweaking, would work well on contemporary scripts too. Then, if I were to work on a song, or give a presentation in front of a group of people, I'd mark those scripts as well.

See? (This is what's on my notes when I'm teaching in person!)

It dawned on me that this kind of notation, with a little tweaking, would work well on contemporary scripts, too, and then, if I were to work on a song, or give a presentation in front of a group of people, I'd mark those scripts, too.

Soon, I began teaching this "Penning" method to all my students, and they've relied on it to book themselves work in theatre, film, and television; to be cast in audiobooks; and to get them into college and grad school.

I have always wanted to write a book describing the technique, and now, with the advent of publishing on demand, I can reach far more people than I ever could individually, and help actors all over the world create confident, memorable performances in minutes.

I can't wait to share with you the technique I've been honing for decades, which has led me to a successful career as an award-winning actress and audiobook narrator.

So, now that you know all about *me*…

LET'S GET STARTED!

THE PENNING METHOD
for the Panicked Actor

MODULE ONE

FIND YOUR "10"
and The Emotional Rollercoaster

By the end of this course, you (in a panicked moment), will be able to break down your text quickly, so it will be unique to you.

You'll have little guide marks along the way so that you can walk right into an audition and do your best work, and leave knowing that you gave it your all in the room.

Usually when you have very little time to prepare, the tendency is to panic. All logic and reason goes out the window. Your fight, flight, or freeze response kicks in.

You think, "Oh no! I usually work on my monologues for weeks and take them to my coaches and rehearse them over and over and over again. How am I going to figure this out in five minutes?"

You calm yourself (as much as you can). You look over the script, make a ton of great decisions... and then adrenaline takes over. You forget everything you wanted to do, and you end up beating yourself up after you walk out of the room.

(Does this sound familiar?)

Or, you agonize over every single moment and you get flustered and you want to do it over again because it wasn't quite right, and you lose your breath and your nerves get in the way.

(If you're anything like the actor that I am, that is.)

When I started to commit my first instincts to the <u>paper</u> instead of to my <u>memory</u>, however, it freed me up to live in the moment and just PLAY.

To help teach you The Penning Method, we'll be using 12 lines that Lysander speaks in Shakespeare's **A Midsummer Night's Dream**. I'll reference this piece throughout the book.

Feel free to write all over this text as we go - here and/or each time it appears on the page. I've also printed several copies in the back of this book for you to try different choices and compare which you like better.

Write all over it, make big choices, erase, make different choices - hey, this is YOUR book, go for it!

LYSANDER

I am, my lord, as well derived as he,
As well possess'd; my love is more than his;
My fortunes every way as fairly rank'd,
If not with vantage, as Demetrius';
And, which is more than all these boasts can be,
I am beloved of beauteous Hermia:
Why should not I then prosecute my right?
Demetrius, I'll avouch it to his head,
Made love to Nedar's daughter, Helena,
And won her soul; and she, sweet lady, dotes,
Devoutly dotes, dotes in idolatry,
Upon this spotted and inconstant man.

To use this technique with *any* piece, make sure you'll be able to mark on your script somehow. If you're working digitally, that can be with the markup function on your phone or tablet, or you can print it out and mark it in pencil, pen, colored markers — however it works for you, just so long as you're able to physically <u>mark</u> the text.

Got your pencil?

Okay, let's go.

STEP ONE

FIND YOUR "10"
the Top of the Rollercoaster

If I could only tell you ONE thing, it's this:

Before your next audition, no matter how little time you have to prepare, if you do NOTHING else...

Find. Your. 10.

What does that mean, "Find your 10?"

To be able to commit your instincts to the <u>paper</u> (instead of your memory) and free yourself up to live in the moment and just play, it starts with finding your "10."

Think of your emotions like a roller coaster... Where is the most _intense_ moment in your piece? <u>That's</u> your 10.

Now, intense does not have to mean loud or angry. Sometimes the most intense moment is a whispered, heartfelt, _"I love you."_ Maybe it's the happiest you've ever been in your life!

What's the most important point you make in this piece? Find it and mark it.

You can usually find that 10 pretty quickly. Don't be afraid to shift it, though.

You can absolutely change your mind – that's why pencils have erasers! But remember that your first instincts are usually the right ones. Just make a choice and go with it.

Pause here until you've had a chance to find and mark your 10.

⏸ PAUSE HERE

FIND YOUR "10"
Mark it on the margin

LYSANDER

I am, my lord, as well derived as he,
As well possess'd: my love is more than his;
My fortunes every way as fairly rank'd,
If not with vantage, as Demetrius';
And, which is more than all these boasts can be,
I am beloved of beauteous Hermia:
Why should not I then prosecute my right?
Demetrius, I'll avouch it to his head,
Made love to Nedar's daughter, Helena,
And won her soul; and she, sweet lady, dotes,
Devoutly dotes, dotes in idolatry,
Upon this spotted and inconstant man.

Do you have your 10?

Great — let's move on.

Now, know that your 10 may not be the same 10 as anyone else's 10. The point of finding the most intense moment, is so that you have a "peak" in your piece. Then every other moment can vary in intensity around it. Otherwise, you'll end up delivering your audition on all... one... note. *(booooooooriiiiiing!)*

Also, it doesn't matter if you've done this particular piece before, or even a million times. Look at it *today*. How does it strike you *now*, in the present?

What is the most intense moment that you want to convey *today*, in the room, if you were just handed this and told, "look this over and we'll see you in five minutes."

Now...

On an emotional scale of 1 to 10 (knowing your 10 as you now do):
- What number does your piece *start* at?
- What number do you *end* on?
- What immediately *precedes* your 10?
- Do you build up steadily?
- Do you go back-and-forth in intensity, or does it come out of nowhere?
- What number immediately *follows* your 10?
- Where does it change in between?

All these numbers are <u>in relation to</u> your 10, even if you choose to perform your piece very, very quietly.

So between being completely blank (zero), and being at your "10," where do the moments fall? Mark them on the left side of your text.

The brilliant thing about marking these numbers is that *your* numbers are unlikely to be the same as anyone else's numbers, which *immediately* makes this piece unique to YOU.

Pause here and mark all your intensity numbers on the left-hand margin.

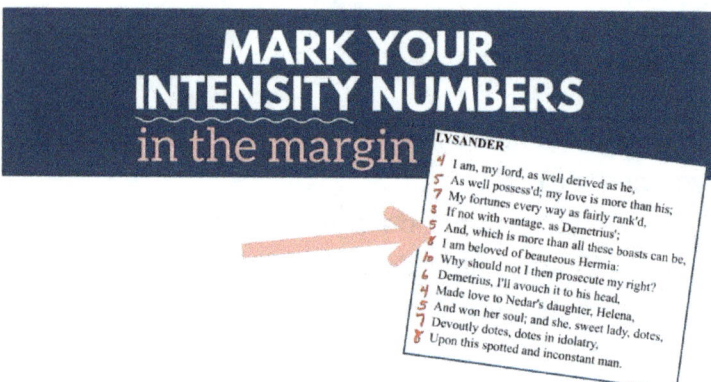

Do you have all your numbers?

Great, let's move on.

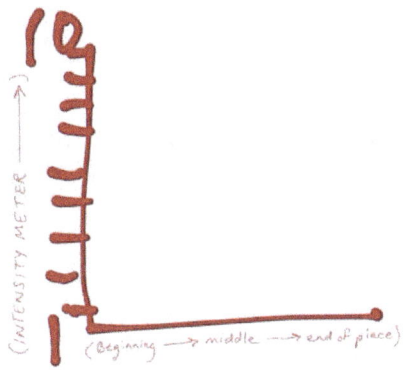

(INTENSITY METER →)

(Beginning → middle → end of piece)

Very quickly draw a messy little X-Y graph — a little right angle, like the one above.

The Y axis on the left is your intensity: 1 to 10. And the X axis on the bottom follows from the beginning of your piece on the left to the end of your piece on the right.

Pause here and plot the numbers you've chosen, in the order you're performing them, on that X-Y graph.

⏸ **PAUSE HERE**

PLOT YOUR NUMBERS
on a quick XY graph

Got your X-Y graph filled out?

Then let's continue.

Now that you have your intensity plotted, <u>connect all the numbers</u>.

What you have here is:

YOUR EMOTIONAL. ROLLERCOASTER.

You'll immediately see how you *get* to your 10, and how you *come down* from it. Unless, of course, it ends up being your last sentence, and then you go out with a BANG!

And what's brilliant about it is that there are no wrong answers. You can do it ANY way.

Actor A and Actor B could vary their emotions in completely different ways, and they're BOTH. CORRECT. They're just unique to *that actor*.

It's a great way to map out your piece visually, intensity-wise. Then if you're overtaken with nerves, you can just visualize where you're supposed to be on your emotional roller coaster.

And it's so quick! You just go dot-dot-dot-dot-dot, and *any way you do it is correct.*

You don't have to vary *widely*. Some roller coasters are kiddie bumps! But you do have to *vary* your emotions to keep them *interesting*.

So maybe you start on a 3 and end on an 8... or perhaps you start on a 6 and end on a 4. But every single "emotional moment" is <u>relative</u> to that 10.

The first thing that will set you apart from any other auditionee is that your piece will <u>not</u> be All. One. Note.

Because the fastest way to turn off a casting director (or a producer or a director or an author or a playwright) is to have where you *start* — and where you *continue* — and where you *end* your audition all come from the <u>same</u> emotional place.

If you YELL IT ALL! Or you don't *play* at all... or everything is on the same stagnant level, you won't get the job.

Use your emotional rollercoaster to take them on an *interesting* ride.

I guarantee that you could put every single actor up for this role in a room and do this exercise with them, and <u>no two actors would map the piece in exactly the same way</u>. There is *no wrong way* to do this.

You have just added <u>uniqueness</u> and <u>specificity</u> to your read that is *text-based* and entirely YOURS.

You now have a <u>map</u>. A *direction* for your read. Or, as my friend Gail noted, you're "building your playground."

And now you can feel free to PLAY within that structure that is uniquely yours.

OK? That's step one!

Even if you only went into your next audition with *this* information, you've already made a huge leap in making your audition stand out from the crowd.

Grab a sip of water and **let's move on to Module Two!**

SEE YOU IN MODULE TWO!

THE PENNING METHOD
for the Panicked Actor

MODULE TWO

RAILROAD TRACKS //
Slashes, / (and Parentheses)

In this entire course, I'm teaching you all the tricks that I've taught my students over the past 30+ years. To score your script in record time so you can relax and play in your auditions, even if you're handed a complex side and told, "look this over and we'll see you in five minutes."

You've already got **your 10**, and built your **emotional rollercoaster**.

Let's move on to Step 2!

STEP TWO

FIND YOUR FULL STOPS
with railroad tracks //

ll these boasts can be,
Hermia:
secute my ...ht?//
his head,
ghter, Helena,
, sweet lady, dotes,
olatry,
nstant man. //

Step 2 — Find Your Full Stops.

Look at this piece again:

LYSANDER

> I am, my lord, as well derived as he,
> As well possess'd; my love is more than his;
> My fortunes every way as fairly rank'd,
> If not with vantage, as Demetrius';
> And, which is more than all these boasts can be,
> I am beloved of beauteous Hermia:
> Why should not I then prosecute my right?
> Demetrius, I'll avouch it to his head,
> Made love to Nedar's daughter, Helena,
> And won her soul; and she, sweet lady, dotes,
> Devoutly dotes, dotes in idolatry,
> Upon this spotted and inconstant man.

Would you be surprised if I told you it's only TWO sentences?

This piece is only two sentences. It's 12 lines long, but it's *only two sentences.*

This is why it's important to mark where your full stops are. Where are the ends of your COMPLETE thoughts?

For this notation, **use a Double Slash: //**

I call it a "railroad track" because it's either:
- at the end of the sentence (you're stopping your "train" of thought)
  or

- a shift so hard it "stops you in your tracks."

The end of *one* complete thought, and the beginning of a *new* one.

Look at the Lysander piece again, and mark your two full stops.

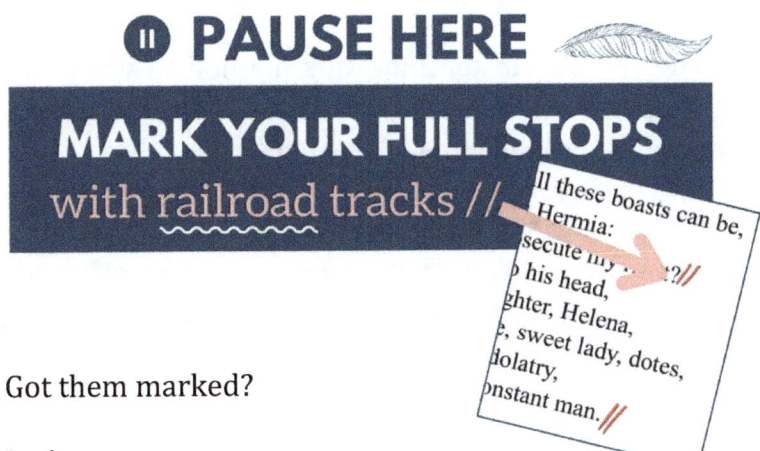

Got them marked?

Let's move on.

The only two full stops in this piece are at the end of "prosecute my right," and after "inconstant man." Those are the ends of the only two sentences in this entire piece.

As a side note — I'm beginning with Shakespearean verse because I have done 54 productions of 23 of The Bard's plays (as of this publication), and that is the basis for this entire method. I learned how to mark up my script starting with Shakespeare. Many of you taking this course may have learned marking

Shakespearean scripts in school as well, but it may have been a while.

After marking my Shakespeare scripts this way for so long, I realized that I could transfer these notations over into contemporary material as well, and it opened up a whole new world for me. I use this method on everything now.

The reason I'm teaching this method to <u>you</u> using Shakespeare, however, is because it's *immediately* easy to see how it helps within the text.

I'm going to show you an audition I did a while back. It was so complex! There were parentheticals inside of parentheticals and incredibly long sentences, and I'm *so glad* I have this method. *(Phew!)*

Something amazing happened on Court #2 of the New Sunshine Golf and Tennis Club just before lunchtime on the day after New Year's, although it was amazing to only one person, namely Loretta Plansky, a seventy-one-year-old widow of solid build and the only female player in the whole club with a one-handed backhand. She and her partner, a new member Mrs. Plansky had met just before stepping on the court that morning and whose name she had failed to retain even though she'd repeated it several times to herself as they shook hands, were playing in the weekly match between the New Sunshiners and the team from Old Sunshine Country Club, the hoity-toitier of the two, dating all the way back to 1989. Mrs. Plansky had been something of a tomboy as a kid, actually playing Little League baseball and Peewee hockey on boys' teams, but she hadn't taken up tennis until she'd married Norm, so although her strokes were effective they weren't much to look at. The third set tiebreak, Mrs. Plansky and her partner receiving, the better of the opponents, a tall blond woman perhaps fifteen years younger than the others, lofted a pretty lob over Mrs. Plansky, a lob with a touch of topspin that was going to land inside the baseline for a clean winner. Mrs. Plansky wheeled around, chased after the ball, and with her back half-turned to the net flicked a backhand down the unguarded alley. Game, set, match. A nice shot, mostly luck, and not the amazing part. The amazing part was that Mrs. Plansky had wheeled around without giving it the slightest thought, she'd simply

From Mrs. Plansky's Revenge by Peter Abrahams (aka Spencer Quinn)
reprinted with permission

That <u>entire page</u> is only *eight* sentences. And you see those two highlighted segments? The bottom phrase is the *continuation* of that sentence. "She and her partner… were playing in the weekly match" is the actual sentence, but look at all that stuff in between! So the marks kept me on track in explaining the throughline of the story.

OK! So you've got your railroad tracks marked, and in this piece there were only two.

If there had been a sentence in the middle of the piece that was interrupted, like in *The Princess Bride* when Vizzini diverts The Man in Black's attention by saying, "And I choose…// What in the world could THAT be?" Even though there's not a period or an exclamation point or a question mark at the break, it would *also* merit a railroad track.

A shift like that completely stops the thought you were *going* to say, and moves you onto *another* thought. Make sense?

OK, moving on.

STEP THREE

THE SINGLE / SLASH
for breaths and phrasing

LYSANDER

I am, my lord,/as well derived as he/
As well ...s'd/my love is more than his/
If not ... every way as fairly rank'd ./
And, ...atch is more than as Demetrius';
I am beloved of beauteous Hermia:
Why should not I then prosecute my right?/
Demetrius, I'll avouch it to his head,
Made love to Nedar's daughter, Helena,
And won her soul; and she, sweet lady, dotes,
Devoutly dotes, dotes in idolatry,
Upon this spotted and inconstant man.//

This next step is the marking
that helps me out more than anything:

Step 3 — The Single Slash.

Notated like so: /

The single slash breaks up your phrases. You want to use it:

- anywhere you could possibly *breathe*
- to add *clarity* to convoluted sentences and
- to keep thoughts and phrases separated

So go through Lysander's speech and mark the slashes where you could possibly *(naturally)* breathe.

Now, this doesn't mean you *have* to breathe every time you put a slash (otherwise, you'd be hyperventilating: "I am, [BREATH] my Lord [BREATH] as well derived as he [BREATH]…" — and you would pass out in the middle of your audition. Not what we're going for!

If you *are* losing your breath and <u>panicking</u> in the room, by marking those possible breathing places, you have given yourself multiple pause points where you can collect yourself and take a *natural* breath. You don't have to get all the way to the end of a sentence that is seven lines long to refill your lungs with oxygen.

And again, *your* marks will be different from anyone else's marks; for example, on "why should 'not I' then prosecute my right?" I have a tendency to invert things that are syntactically different from the way I speak. If I weren't paying attention, I could very well say, "why should 'I not' then prosecute my right?"

In Shakespeare's verse, written in iambic pentameter, you don't *normally* stress your personal pronouns, but that 'I' is on a stressed iamb.

And I would almost always flip it.

In my own notation of this piece, I actually have slashes in between "not" and "I," and *after* "I." So that I visually <u>see</u> a potential tongue-tripping hazard as it's coming up. "Why should not/ I/" — It's a bolded cue telling me that I need to pay attention to that phrase and say the word order correctly.

These slashes are also useful anywhere you want to add clarity to convoluted sentences, or to keep thoughts and phrases separated.

But the *first* place to think about is where you could breathe.

Again, there are NO. WRONG. ANSWERS. And that's the reason why I love this so much. Yours is different than mine, and that's why we do this! Because you should be memorable for *your* choices and not for, "This is the 'right' way to do it," because THAT DOESN'T EXIST. The people watching want to see *your unique way* of doing it.

So take your time, go through and mark your single slashes throughout the script, and pause the lesson here until you have that completed.

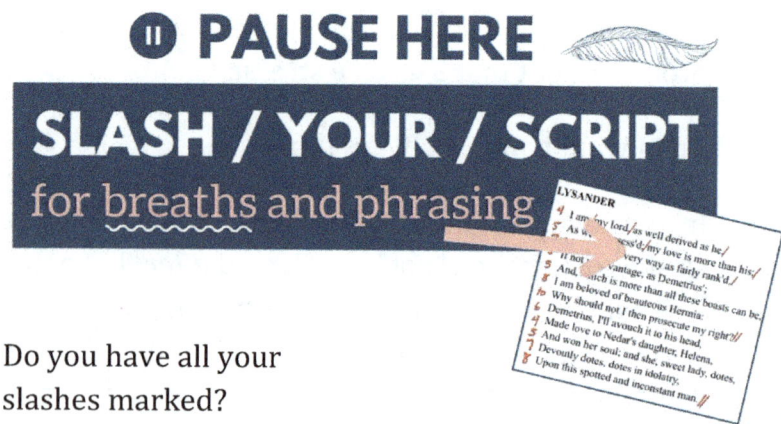

Do you have all your slashes marked?

OK, cool!

Now we're going to move on to...

STEP FOUR

(PARENTHETICALS)
asides from the main point

Step 4 — Parentheticals.

Parentheses ( ) are used to delineate any phrases that would be considered an *aside* from the end point of your sentence.

For example, "I'll avouch it to his head," makes a great parenthetical. Because the sentence is, "Demetrius... made love to Nedar's daughter Helena." But the *aside* from the end point of that phrase is, "I'll avouch it to his head." So that might be in parentheses in your markings.

Imagine you are <u>driving a train through your sentence</u>. Where would be a place where you *look out the window*?

Again, there are <u>no wrong choices</u>. There is nothing wrong with the way *you* do it versus the way *I* do it. It makes us unique. And we don't want to all do it the same way, right? That's why we're doing this method!

Think of parentheticals like <u>spice</u>. Just a *little* bit in there. (Unless you're doing that one audition I showed you before with parentheticals within parentheticals!)

I'm <u>driving a train</u> through my sentence, but I'm *looking out the window* on (this phrase).

Go through your piece, and figure out where you might use a parenthetical or a few, and when you're done, turn the page for **Module Three**!

(Mark Your Parentheticals First)

THE PENNING METHOD
for the Panicked Actor

SEE YOU IN MODULE THREE!

MODULE THREE

The added advantage of marking your script is that little bits of the speech are being embedded in your memory with each pass. By the time you've marked everything, you're so familiar with the piece, the words are second nature.

Nerves will try to take the words from you (lol), but with your markings and the understanding that you've gleaned thus far, you'll be able to "speak the speech," even if Anxiety rears its frazzled head.

So far, you've found your **10**, and built your **Emotional Rollercoaster**. You know where your **Full Stops** are, and you know **where you can Breathe**. You've **broken up any problematic phrasing**, also noting **Parentheticals** where you're *(looking out the window)* as you're driving a train through your sentence to your point.

STEP FIVE

①-②-③s

lists or sequences

Step 5 — 1-2-3's.

Now comedy, we all know, comes in threes, right? Very often authors or playwrights or speechwriters will list three things in a row.

For instance, "we do <u>this</u> (1), and then we do <u>this</u> (2), and then we do <u>this</u> (3)."

You want to make sure that, whenever you have a list like that, use the 1-2-3's to signal to your brain — "we have a sequence coming up!"

The act of *listing* the items usually comes with a shift in *pitch* on each.

This **first** thing, then this **next** thing, then this **third** thing, and it's usually pitched either:

- normal-high-lower

    or
- normal-low-higher

Just make sure that the pitch *varies* on those three things.

It doesn't have to be just three, there might be more (but it's usually three). In Lysander's first sentence, you could make a case for marking the five points of why he's better than Demetrius, to help keep your mind straight on your argument.

I like to write the number in a circle above the word I'm going to stress.

Go ahead and pause here to see if you want to make any 1-2-3 notations in this piece, then continue after you've marked your text.

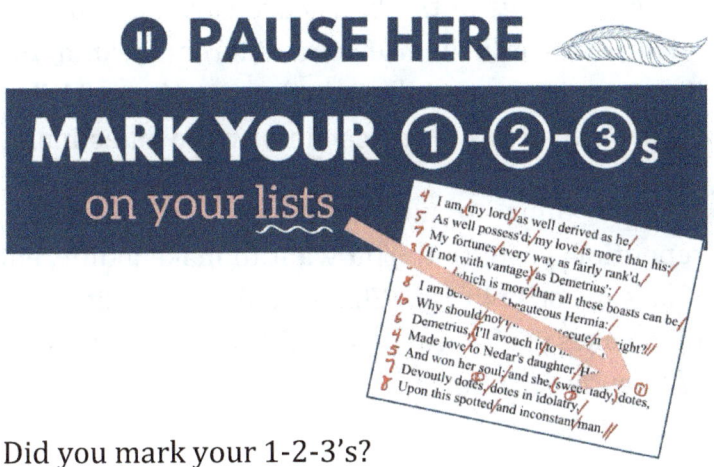

Did you mark your 1-2-3's?

And again, you could do 1-2-3-4-5, you can do it up to 18 or whatever. But ordering them gives your brain a signal that they're connected.

A side note of things to pay attention to with lists: each item you're listing is <u>different</u> from the last. Make sure it *sounds* like you have a different connection for each word.

In this piece, "derived," "possessed," "ranked," and "beloved" are four <u>different</u> things.

1. I'm DERIVED from the same class of family.
2. I'm POSSESSED of (or I have) the same kind of things that he has. (I have a house, I have a car, etc.)
3. My fortunes are RANKED just as high as his, and maybe I have more than he does!
4. And I am BELOVED of beauteous Hermia.

All those things in the list? Make sure that you are giving the words themselves a different meaning, so it doesn't just sound like a listicle, you know? What each word means *to you* can inform the inflection.

Another thing to pay attention to is repetition, repetition, repetition. You want to make a different *choice* in each phrase. What is it about this situation that makes you repeat yourself? What are you saying *differently* each time?

For example: "Dotes" is different from "DEVOUTLY dotes," which is different from "Dotes in IDOLATRY."

And that moves us perfectly into...

STEP SIX

THE UNDERLINE
for stressed syllables

Step 6 — The Underline!

You may have heard that Shakespeare uses a meter in his verse called *iambic pentameter*, right? It's five 'iambs' which are stressed "ba-DUM," in a row.

But what you may not know is that not only do iambs mimic the human heartbeat:

ba-*dum*, ba-*dum*, ba-*dum*, ba-*dum*, ba-*dum*

but...

it's *still* the *way* we *most*-ly *speak* to-*day*.

Use *under**lines*** to *mark* the *words* that *help* you *make* your *point*.

So because the speech is iambic pentameter, go ahead and underline the stressed iambs: ba-_dum_, ba-_dum_, ba-_dum_, ba-_dum_, ba-_dum_. I _am_ my _Lord_ as _well_ de-_rived_ as _he_... and go on from there.

Again, you may have studied iambic pentameter in college or even in high school using Shakespeare's texts. But learning this stressed-word technique will help you with contemporary pieces as well.

Side note — in a quick five-minute breakdown, even if you know more about Shakespearean meter, don't worry about "spondees" and "trochees" and all the extra-fancy bits. Just underline it as if it were straight iambic pentameter, and figure out where to elide vowels together. The _stressed words_ are the most important right now.

In a contemporary piece, you would figure out your stresses where you would emphasize them naturally. In this case for Shakespeare, I want you to also figure out how you would say it naturally to make the stresses work in _your_ voice.

Now note: this is *not* a Shakespeare course. This is a text-marking course. And if you were working with a contemporary piece right now, everybody's markings would be different.

But if you're writing a speech, and you decide that you want to say, "Our company has taken off this year..."

Our <u>com</u>-pa-<u>ny</u> has <u>ta</u>-ken <u>off</u> this <u>year</u>...

It's iambic pentameter! So it's very useful to know this. And in Shakespearean verse, it's also easy to see how the stressed words work.

So pause here and underline the stressed words.

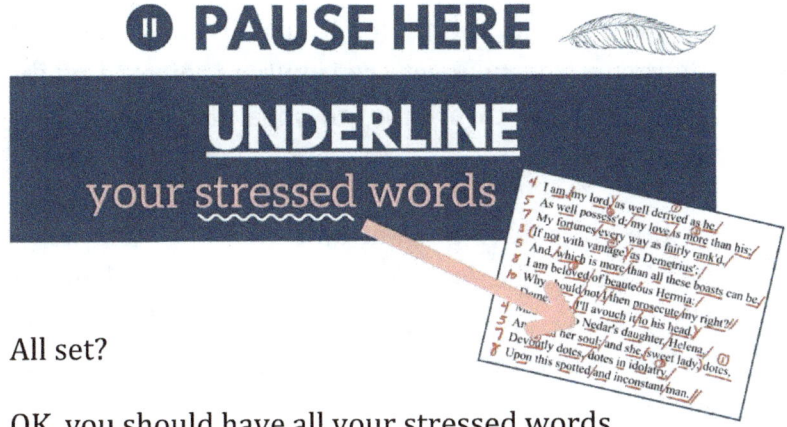

All set?

OK, you should have all your stressed words marked now.

Again, I just want to emphasize there is no *wrong* way to do this. If you want to use multiple colors so you can see all the different options, go for it! I do it all in one color because I'm imagining I'm in an audition room and I have five minutes to go through this and I only have a pencil. When I'm teaching this course live, I mark the text in red so it's easier to see on my slides.

Something to note here: if what you're auditioning for is Shakespearean verse like this, pay attention to the <u>ends</u> of each line. You see this one ends in all *stressed* syllables. It's very straight and metered.

But in any other Shakespearean verse piece, note which lines do NOT end in a stressed word. That's known as a "feminine ending." How often does it happen?

If there's a <u>lot</u> of them, it usually indicates the character is very upset or off-kilter, indicated by the way you have to breathe to speak in a meter that flows erratically.

In this, Lysander is calm and measured. He has a good case, and he's making it to her father: "I am the right man for the job, and he's not." He's not "freaking out" in a way that indicates he doesn't have his case prepared.

So let's move on to…

STEP SEVEN

THE SQUIGGLE
for words you want to CHEW

Step 7 — The SQUIGGLE.

The squiggle is what you use under a word you REALLY want to CHEW. Underline your word with a squiggly line to mark it for *extra emphasis,* or driving an opinion into the listener's ear.

Now, if you think about people "chewing the scenery," that's usually over the top (and not a complimentary thing to say about another actor.) They chew their lines too much, on <u>EVERY</u>... <u>*WORD*</u>. But again, this is spice. We want to add in a little bit of salt, a little bit of pepper, a little bit of cayenne. Not dump the whole can into the mix.

Which are the words in the piece that you *really* want to CHEW? There is no grammatical structure as to what kind of words they have to be, though it should already be one of the words you intend to stress. It wouldn't make sense to chew a word that's not stressed.

Squiggle under any of the stressed words that you want to just _maul_ with your mouth. And by mauling, I mean eeeeeeextra draaaaaawn-ouuuuuut and _really_ hitting the consonants and the vowels, because that is the word that you truly, desperately want to _drive_ into the listener's ear.

And again, it's important to note that you can change your mind.

You can _always_ change your mind.

Go through and find any words that you would like to chew, and then grab a sip of water, and we'll start **Module Four**!

SQUIGGLE words you want to CHEW, then...

SEE YOU IN MODULE FOUR!

MODULE FOUR

"QUOTATION MARKS"
[Brackets], and Verbs

THAT'S ALL!

So you've got your **"10,"** your **emotional rollercoaster**, your **full stops** and **phrasing**, your **lists** noted, your **stressed words**, and your ***REALLY stressed words***.

If we were in an in-person group right now, I'd have everyone hold up their paper to take a quick glance at all the markings of the rest of the people in the class. We're all marking the same text — up for the same role, as it were — but with these markings, our reads are totally *unique* to us.

If you find yourself hesitating on a mark, thinking you're going to make a "wrong" choice, I'll tell you — just go with your first instincts. If it makes sense to how you want to portray the role, "wrong" doesn't exist — an unusual choice will just spark a discussion of why you chose to take it that particular way. Just voice your opinion if they ask.

Speaking of which: you should ALWAYS have an opinion of *every single thing that comes out of your mouth*. Nothing that comes out of your mouth was meant to be thrown away *without thinking.*

CHOOSE your words. You didn't <u>know</u> you were going to say this. Why did you?

I've seen people in auditions miss opportunities by glossing over or rushing past lines because they think those particular words aren't important to what the character is trying to convey. Don't do that.

There *are* reasons that people use "throwaway" lines: to deflect attention, or to underplay the importance of information, or to mislead another character. If you're going to throw it away, why did you *choose* to throw it away?

Everything that comes out of your mouth was <u>agonized</u> over by the playwright, or the author, or the person who wrote the speech or song. There is nothing that should be thrown away *without thought.*

So always, always, always have an opinion. For *everything*.

Got it?

Then let's keep going!

STEP EIGHT

"QUOTATION MARKS"
to point up people or ideas

Step 8 — "Quotation marks."

Use quotation marks where you want to set something apart, as if with "air quotes," or if you're introducing a person or a concept for the first time, so that you have a visual to "point it up" in the piece.

Something to note: if you are given a piece that has Capitalized Words that are not proper names — it indicates a personification of a thing or idea: "Time," "Death," anything like that.

Even if you're working on a contemporary piece a random Capitalized Word might occur — it means that the author either made an editorial error (haha), or they wanted that particular idea or name or thought to be *emphasized* in some way.

Pause here and see if there are any places that you want to use "air quotes" or setting up a person or an idea that you're introducing for the first time.

USE "QUOTATION MARKS"
to point up people or ideas

> y fortunes every way as fairly rank'd,
> not with vantage, as Demetrius',
> hd, which is more than all these boasts
> m beloved of beauteous Hermia:
> si uld not I then prosecute my rig
> me I'll avouch it to his head,
> ue love to Nedar's daughter, Helena,
> hd won her soul; and she, sweet lady, d
> vcutly dotes, dotes in idolatry,
> oon this spotted and inconstant man.

You've got your quotation marks set down?

(Again, there are <u>no wrong answers</u> here. These marks are for you and you alone. Everybody's markings will be different, and *that's the point*.)

If you have an "air quote" phrase, or if you're introducing a person or a concept for the first time, quotation marks signal to your mind, "oh right, I'm supposed to make sure they hear the name, or that thing, because the audience hasn't heard it before." You want to make sure they pay attention!

Almost to the end! Moving on to...

[BRACKET] BEAT SHIFTS
in the margin

Step 9 — [Bracketing] your beat shifts.

Some people like to start breaking down a script with their beat shifts. But if you're given a piece and told, "go out in the hallway and learn this in five minutes," I've found Steps 1-8 more valuable for me to do *first*, so that you really know where your shifts *happen*.

- How many <u>ideas</u> do you have in this piece?
- Where do you *shift* them?
- Where do you change your tactics?
- Where do you discover something new?

The piece is a long path, but it's not a straight line. (That's boring.) Where are the forks in the road?

Mark where your ideas *shift* on the outside of your emotional rollercoaster numbers by using brackets.

Pause here and pick back up when you've got all your brackets in.

[BRACKET] BEAT SHIFTS
in the margin

Do you have your
beats marked?

You may also choose to mark them into even smaller
"mini beats" as well — whatever helps YOU.

Moving on to the final step!

STEP TEN

CIRCLE YOUR VERBS
and don't forget
am, are, is, was, were!

Step 10 — The Verbs.

Your verbs are the *engine*
that drives you through the piece.

Go through and circle *all* of them.

Your verbs will almost always be some of your underlined words as well. You should be able to tell the *meat* of the whole story using only the inflection you use on your verbs.

Pause here and circle all your verbs — don't forget the helping verbs: am, are, is, was, were — and then we'll move on.

Did you circle all your verbs?

Remember here that Shakespeare's syntax is wonky — "am derived" and "am possessed" are the whole verbs, even though they're split in the phrasing.

What do I mean about telling the *meat* of the story with just the verbs?

Read this through, out loud, with *deep meaning* behind each word. You'll be able to understand the story, even though there are no other words spoken but the verbs:

- am... derived
- possessed
- is
- ranked
- is... be:
- am beloved!
- should prosecute!
- avouch:
- made love
- won
- dotes, dotes, dotes!

You can *hear* it, right? Your verbs are the *engine* that drives you through the piece.

So, with all your verbs done, **those are all the marks!**

THAT'S ALL!

THE PENNING METHOD
for the Panicked Actor

YOU DID IT!

THE PENNING METHOD
for the Panicked Actor

Congratulations! You now have a whole new set of tools to help you in panicked, last-minute audition situations.

Simple, right? But so powerful, and so helpful when your brain is on overdrive.

I'd love to see your piece if you want to privately share it. You can take a photo of your markings, or you can video yourself performing this piece as if you were auditioning, using your marks, then upload it and share it with me at:
support@panickedactor.com.

I also coach privately if you'd like to work more deeply — or if you've got a big audition coming up or a big speech to prepare and you'd like to work with me one-on-one.

I've been teaching this breakdown method for over 30 years, to hundreds of students. The Penning Method *works*.

People have used it to get parts in films and on television, to audition for Broadway and audiobooks, to get into grad school or college.

They've used it to calm their nerves when they're auditioning for a new producer. Or a new director. Or when they're feeling stuck with a piece, or need to breathe new life into an old monologue.

Know that all of these are TOOLS to keep your choices visible. You can use as many or as few of these as help you, and in any order that works for you, so you can go into your audition or your booking and just PLAY.

As I said before, my friend Gail refers to this as 'building the playground.'

And if you're anything like me, when your adrenaline ramps up, and you're in front of a person in power whose opinion of your performance can get you a job, it's easy to start shaking and lose your breath.

All the brilliant ideas you came up with in the hall go right out the window. And again, most of the panic comes from the fear that you'll freeze up and forget.

But by quickly sketching out these landmarks in your script, you can SEE the handholds and the jumping spots.

You don't have to rely on your <u>memory</u> in the room because all your decisions are RIGHT THERE.

You can relax and *play*, because you know you won't lose your place, you know what you're doing, and your performance will be memorable, interesting, and UNIQUE to YOU.

And most of all, you'll be able to walk out of the audition with your head held high rather than smacking your forehead going, "Oh no! I meant to… (*whatever*)!"

And you'll go grab a beverage, or a treat of your choice, because you <u>knew</u> what you were doing, you <u>showed</u> them your best work, and you did everything you <u>wanted</u> to do IN THE ROOM.

Because, for heaven's sake, we're the only people lucky enough to PLAY for a living!

But if the monkey bars are <u>invisible</u>, how can you confidently *swing* and *flip* and wow them with the showstopping performance you *know* you're capable of delivering?

With this method, you go into the room, and the nice thing is, it's all right there.

<u>There's</u> your playground.

All YOU have to do… is *play*.

PENNING METHOD CHEAT SHEET

1) Find your "10" & Emotional Rollercoaster numbers in the margin

2) Railroad-track your Full Stops. //

3) Slash / for phrasing / and breathing

4) (Mark your Parentheticals)

5) Visualize your Lists with ① - ② - ③'s

6) Underline your Stressed Syllables

7) Squiggle words to CHEW

8) Point up "Air Quotes" & "New People" or "Ideas"

9) [Bracket] your beats

10) Circle verbs

Then trust the marks and PLAY!

APPENDIX:
SAMPLE MARKINGS FOR EACH STEP

LYSANDER

I am, my lord, as well derived as he,
As well possess'd; my love is more than his;
My fortunes every way as fairly rank'd,
If not with vantage, as Demetrius';
And, which is more than all these boasts can be,
I am beloved of beauteous Hermia:
Why should not I then prosecute my right?
Demetrius, I'll avouch it to his head,
Made love to Nedar's daughter, Helena,
And won her soul; and she, sweet lady, dotes,
Devoutly dotes, dotes in idolatry,
Upon this spotted and inconstant man.

STEP 1:
FIND YOUR 10

Remember... this is only <u>one person</u>'s idea of how to mark the script. There is no <u>right</u> way. Your markings may look different, and that's okay! This is just for illustrative purposes.

LYSANDER

> I am, my lord, as well derived as he,
> As well possess'd; my love is more than his;
> My fortunes every way as fairly rank'd,
> If not with vantage, as Demetrius';
> And, which is more than all these boasts can be,
> I am beloved of beauteous Hermia:
> *10* Why should not I then prosecute my right?
> Demetrius, I'll avouch it to his head,
> Made love to Nedar's daughter, Helena,
> And won her soul; and she, sweet lady, dotes,
> Devoutly dotes, dotes in idolatry,
> Upon this spotted and inconstant man.

STEP 1:
THE EMOTIONAL ROLLERCOASTER

Remember... this is only <u>one person</u>'s idea of how to mark the script. There is no <u>right</u> way. Your markings may look different, and that's okay! This is just for illustrative purposes.

LYSANDER

4   I am, my lord, as well derived as he,
5   As well possess'd; my love is more than his;
7   My fortunes every way as fairly rank'd,
3   If not with vantage, as Demetrius';
5   And, which is more than all these boasts can be,
8   I am beloved of beauteous Hermia:
10   Why should not I then prosecute my right?
6   Demetrius, I'll avouch it to his head,
4   Made love to Nedar's daughter, Helena,
5   And won her soul; and she, sweet lady, dotes,
7   Devoutly dotes, dotes in idolatry,
8   Upon this spotted and inconstant man.

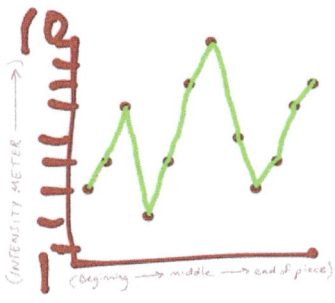

(INTENSITY METER →)

(beginning → middle → end of piece)

STEP 2:
FULL STOPS

Remember... this is only <u>one person's</u> idea of how to mark the script. There is no <u>right</u> way. Your markings may look different, and that's okay! This is just for illustrative purposes.

LYSANDER

4 I am, my lord, as well derived as he,
5 As well possess'd; my love is more than his;
7 My fortunes every way as fairly rank'd,
3 If not with vantage, as Demetrius';
5 And, which is more than all these boasts can be,
8 I am beloved of beauteous Hermia:
10 Why should not I then prosecute my right?//
6 Demetrius, I'll avouch it to his head,
4 Made love to Nedar's daughter, Helena,
5 And won her soul; and she, sweet lady, dotes,
7 Devoutly dotes, dotes in idolatry,
8 Upon this spotted and inconstant man.//

STEP 3:
SLASH YOUR SCRIPT

Remember... this is only <u>one person</u>'s idea of how to mark the script. There is no <u>right</u> way. Your markings may look different, and that's okay! This is just for illustrative purposes.

4 I am,/my lord,/as well derived as he./
5 As well possess'd;/my love/is more than his;/
7 My fortunes/every way as fairly rank'd,/
3 If not with vantage,/as Demetrius';/
5 And,/which is more/than all these boasts can be,/
8 I am beloved/of beauteous Hermia:/
10 Why should/not/I/then prosecute/my right?//
6 Demetrius,/I'll avouch it/to his head,/
4 Made love/to Nedar's daughter,/Helena,/
5 And won her soul;/and she, sweet lady, dotes,
7 Devoutly dotes,/dotes in idolatry,/
8 Upon this spotted/and inconstant/man. //

STEP 4:
PARENTHETICALS

Remember... this is only <u>one person</u>'s idea of how to mark the script. There is no <u>right</u> way. Your markings may look different, and that's okay! This is just for illustrative purposes.

4   I am, (my lord,) as well derived as he. /
5   As well possess'd; /my love /is more than his; /
7   My fortunes /every way as fairly rank'd, /
3   (If not with vantage) as Demetrius'; /
5   And, /which is more /than all these boasts can be, /
8   I am beloved /of beauteous Hermia: /
10 Why should /not /I /then prosecute /my right? //
6   Demetrius, /I'll avouch it /to his head, /
4   Made love /to Nedar's daughter, /Helena, /
5   And won her soul; /and she, (sweet lady,) dotes,
7   Devoutly dotes, /dotes in idolatry, /
8   Upon this spotted /and inconstant /man. //

STEP FIVE:
1-2-3's

Remember... this is only <u>one person</u>'s idea of how to mark the script. There is no <u>right</u> way. Your markings may look different, and that's okay! This is just for illustrative purposes.

4 I am, my lord, as well derived as he, ①

5 As well possess'd; my love is more than his; ③

7 My fortunes every way as fairly rank'd, ④

3 (If not with vantage) as Demetrius';

5 And, which is more than all these boasts can be, ⑤

8 I am beloved of beauteous Hermia:

10 Why should not I then prosecute my right? //

6 Demetrius, I'll avouch it to his head,

4 Made love to Nedar's daughter, Helena, ①

5 And won her soul; and she, (sweet lady,) dotes,

7 Devoutly dotes, ② dotes in idolatry, ③

8 Upon this spotted and inconstant man. //

STEP 6:
UNDERLINE YOUR STRESSED WORDS

Remember... this is only <u>one person</u>'s idea of how to mark the script. There is no <u>right</u> way. Your markings may look different, and that's okay! This is just for illustrative purposes.

*CAVEAT: In this instance, since Lysander's speech is in iambic pentameter, most people's underlined words <u>would</u> be the same — try an exercise where you underline it differently. How does that change your read?

4 I am, my lord, as well derived as he.

5 As well possess'd; my love is more than his;

7 My fortunes every way as fairly rank'd,

3 (If not with vantage, as Demetrius';

5 And, which is more than all these boasts can be,

8 I am beloved of beauteous Hermia:

10 Why should not I then prosecute my right?

6 Demetrius, I'll avouch it to his head,

4 Made love to Nedar's daughter, Helena,

5 And won her soul; and she, sweet lady, dotes,

7 Devoutly dotes, dotes in idolatry,

8 Upon this spotted and inconstant man.

STEP 7:
SQUIGGLE WORDS TO CHEW

Remember... this is only <u>one person</u>'s idea of how to mark the script. There is no <u>right</u> way. Your markings may look different, and that's okay! This is just for illustrative purposes.

4 I am, my lord, as well derived as he.
5 As well possess'd; my love is more than his;
7 My fortunes every way as fairly rank'd,
3 (If not with vantage, as Demetrius';
5 And, which is more than all these boasts can be,
8 I am beloved of beauteous Hermia:
10 Why should not I then prosecute my right?
6 Demetrius, I'll avouch it to his head,
4 Made love to Nedar's daughter, Helena,
5 And won her soul; and she, sweet lady, dotes,
7 Devoutly dotes, dotes in idolatry,
8 Upon this spotted and inconstant man.

STEP 8:
"QUOTATION MARKS"

Remember... this is only <u>one person</u>'s idea of how to mark the script. There is no <u>right</u> way. Your markings may look different, and that's okay! This is just for illustrative purposes.

4 I am, my lord, as well derived as he.
5 As well possess'd: my love is more than his;
7 My fortunes every way as fairly rank'd,
3 (If not with vantage,) as Demetrius';
5 And, which is more than all these boasts can be
8 I am beloved of beauteous Hermia:
10 Why should not I then prosecute my right?
6 Demetrius, I'll avouch it to his head,
4 Made love to Nedar's daughter, Helena,
5 And won her soul; and she, (sweet lady,) dotes,
7 Devoutly dotes, dotes in idolatry,
8 Upon this spotted and inconstant man.

STEP 9:
BRACKET BEAT SHIFTS

Remember... this is only <u>one person</u>'s idea of how to mark the script. There is no <u>right</u> way. Your markings may look different, and that's okay! This is just for illustrative purposes.

I am, my lord, as well derived as he.
As well possess'd; my love is more than his;
My fortunes every way as fairly rank'd,
(If not with vantage, as Demetrius';
And, which is more than all these boasts can be,
I am beloved of beauteous Hermia:
Why should not I then prosecute my right?
Demetrius, I'll avouch it to his head,
Made love to Nedar's daughter, Helena,
And won her soul; and she, sweet lady, dotes,
Devoutly dotes, dotes in idolatry,
Upon this spotted and inconstant man.

STEP 10:
CIRCLE YOUR VERBS

Remember... this is only <u>one person</u>'s idea of how to mark the script. There is no <u>right</u> way. Your markings may look different, and that's okay! This is just for illustrative purposes.

LYSANDER

I am, my lord, as well derived as he.
As well possess'd; my love is more than his;
My fortunes every way as fairly rank'd,
If not with vantage, as Demetrius';
And, which is more than all these boasts can be,
I am beloved of beauteous Hermia:
Why should not I then prosecute my right?
Demetrius, I'll avouch it to his head,
Made love to Nedar's daughter, Helena,
And won her soul: and she, sweet lady, dotes,
Devoutly dotes, dotes in idolatry,
Upon this spotted and inconstant man.

EXTRA COPIES TO PLAY WITH

Use these additional copies of Lysander's speech if you'd like to try it several different ways, or for more practice, or to try this exercise with friends.

It's your book — your choice!

LYSANDER

> I am, my lord, as well derived as he,
> As well possess'd; my love is more than his;
> My fortunes every way as fairly rank'd,
> If not with vantage, as Demetrius';
> And, which is more than all these boasts can be,
> I am beloved of beauteous Hermia:
> Why should not I then prosecute my right?
> Demetrius, I'll avouch it to his head,
> Made love to Nedar's daughter, Helena,
> And won her soul; and she, sweet lady, dotes,
> Devoutly dotes, dotes in idolatry,
> Upon this spotted and inconstant man.

LYSANDER

I am, my lord, as well derived as he,
As well possess'd; my love is more than his;
My fortunes every way as fairly rank'd,
If not with vantage, as Demetrius';
And, which is more than all these boasts can be,
I am beloved of beauteous Hermia:
Why should not I then prosecute my right?
Demetrius, I'll avouch it to his head,
Made love to Nedar's daughter, Helena,
And won her soul; and she, sweet lady, dotes,
Devoutly dotes, dotes in idolatry,
Upon this spotted and inconstant man.

LYSANDER

I am, my lord, as well derived as he,
As well possess'd; my love is more than his;
My fortunes every way as fairly rank'd,
If not with vantage, as Demetrius';
And, which is more than all these boasts can be,
I am beloved of beauteous Hermia:
Why should not I then prosecute my right?
Demetrius, I'll avouch it to his head,
Made love to Nedar's daughter, Helena,
And won her soul; and she, sweet lady, dotes,
Devoutly dotes, dotes in idolatry,
Upon this spotted and inconstant man.

LYSANDER

I am, my lord, as well derived as he,
As well possess'd; my love is more than his;
My fortunes every way as fairly rank'd,
If not with vantage, as Demetrius';
And, which is more than all these boasts can be,
I am beloved of beauteous Hermia:
Why should not I then prosecute my right?
Demetrius, I'll avouch it to his head,
Made love to Nedar's daughter, Helena,
And won her soul; and she, sweet lady, dotes,
Devoutly dotes, dotes in idolatry,
Upon this spotted and inconstant man.

LYSANDER

I am, my lord, as well derived as he,
As well possess'd; my love is more than his;
My fortunes every way as fairly rank'd,
If not with vantage, as Demetrius';
And, which is more than all these boasts can be,
I am beloved of beauteous Hermia:
Why should not I then prosecute my right?
Demetrius, I'll avouch it to his head,
Made love to Nedar's daughter, Helena,
And won her soul; and she, sweet lady, dotes,
Devoutly dotes, dotes in idolatry,
Upon this spotted and inconstant man.

NOTES

Here's a handy reference card for you to take with you in your wallet, in case you start to panic and forget everything you've learned! You got this!

THE PENNING METHOD
for the Panicked Actor

1) Find your "10" & Emotional Rollercoaster numbers in the margin

2) Railroad-track your Full Stops. //

3) Slash / for phrasing / and breathing

4) (Mark your Parentheticals)

5) Visualize your Lists with ① - ② - ③'s

6) Underline your Stressed Syllables

7) Squiggle words to CHEW

8) Point up "Air Quotes" and "New People or Ideas"

9) [Bracket] your beats

10) Circle verbs

About the Author

Marni Penning (fondly dubbed "The Maven of a Million Voices") comes across as bubbly and friendly, but don't let that twinkle in her eye fool you. Beneath the surface lies depth and range that has propelled her to a successful stage and film career spanning decades.

She's been acting on stage since age 8, including 54 productions of 23 Shakespearean plays (as of this publication), on stages all over the world, and now gets to play ALL the parts as an award-winning audiobook narrator.

Marni developed The Penning Method for her coaching students beginning in 1994, and has refined these techniques over the past several decades into the streamlined version you now hold in your hands. You can find Marni under her moniker "The Lady Hamlet" across all social media.

http://panickedactor.com
http://theladyhamlet.com